One-Room Schoolhouses of Arkansas as Seen through a Pinhole

One-Room Schoolhouses of Arkansas as Seen through a Pinhole

text and photographs by

Thomas Harding

with an afterword by

Cyrus Sutherland

THE UNIVERSITY OF ARKANSAS PRESS • FAYETTEVILLE • 1993

97 96 95 94 93   5 4 3 2 1

This book was designed by John Coghlan using the typeface Simoncini Garamond.

The paper used in this publication meets the minimum requirements of the American
National Standard for Permanence of Paper for Printed Library Materials Z39.48-
1984. ♾

This project was funded in part by the Department of Arkansas Heritage, Arkansas
Power & Light Company, and Entergy Corporation.

Library of Congress Cataloging–in–Publication Data

Harding, Thomas.
        One–room schoolhouses of Arkansas as seen through a pinhole / text and
    photographs by Thomas Harding ; with an afterword by Cyrus Sutherland.
            p.   cm.
        ISBN 1–55728–271–4 (cloth). — ISBN 1–55728–272–2 (pbk.)
        1. Rural schools—Arkansas—Pictorial works. I. Title.
    LB1567.H345   1993
    370.19'346'09767–dc20   92–30060
                                                                             CIP

Photograph of Thomas Harding on p. viii by Bill Parsons.

One-Room Schoolhouses of Arkansas
as Seen through a Pinhole

Contents

Introduction

There is an undefinable but compelling sensation one has upon coming across, in a clearing or along a barren road, a structure that was once a thriving enterprise. Such is the case with the one-room schoolhouses which dot the Arkansas landscape. They assume a variety of architectural forms and are in differing degrees of repair—some, in fact, are in pristine condition while others have collapsed under the weight of age and nature. And yet all have a common element: they contain the traces of a time, not so long ago, when the people of the state began to muster the artifacts of civilization in a centralized place with the distinct mission of passing them on to the next generation.

That generation has since given way to subsequent generations. But it was my hope that through the simple magic of the pinhole camera their singular sense of purpose and the aura that pervades these structures could somehow be preserved.

When I began this project in 1989, the LaRue school was the first on my then very meager list. I had heard that the school was in the Rogers area, but I could not find LaRue on my state highway map. When I called the Rogers Historical Museum, I was assured that LaRue was in the area. The staff person I spoke to, perplexed because she too was unable to find LaRue on her highway map, called the U.S. Corps of Engineers for help. The following day she called to report that LaRue was now under Beaver Lake! However, she thought the old school building had been moved to high ground near the Rocky Branch community.

I was thrilled upon first seeing this tall, imposing white structure glistening in the sun, with the little bell tower standing silently by its side. I bounded up the steps to explore this building's wonderful photographic possibilities. I peered through a glass panel in the door and was enchanted with what I saw. Here were the old type of student desk, the teacher's desk, blackboards, and hanging maps.

However, both doors were locked. I began photographing the exterior. I then noticed two men in a pickup truck watching me. When I asked them about getting inside the school, they directed me to the postmistress, who, in turn, directed me to Mrs. Ella Mae Stell, who had recently moved to Hobbs, New Mexico. Mrs. Stell returns each year to paint and spruce up the schoolhouse and was responsible for having it moved with all the furnishings including the outhouse to the high ground of Rocky Branch.

After four weeks of trying to reach Mrs. Stell, my persistence paid off. I told her that I desperately wanted to record the interior of the school and asked if she would send me the key. Happy to help, she explained that she had left the key with Mrs. Judy Duguid in the Copper Mine community. Two weeks later I met Mrs. Duguid at the school and the key she thought was to the school would not fit. On a wild chance, she opened the glove compartment in her car and pulled out another set of keys. "Let's try these," she said. Sure enough, one of them opened the lock. All of this took three trips from Little Rock, a dozen or so long distance phone calls, and a lot of patience, but it was worth it.

The second schoolhouse I photographed was equally impressive, though on a smaller scale. The Hulsey Bend school can be seen from a mile or so away. This dark red building trimmed in white is backed by the pecan and cypress trees like a ruby on green velvet. The school is owned by Bill Freeze, who has done a splendid job of maintaining it. He welcomes visitors by leaving the doors unlocked and suggesting that they sign the register. The schoolroom is furnished with the teacher's saddle, and a water keg, and books on the desks.

One day after leaving the Clinton area, I drove Highway 95 down to Scotland in search of another schoolhouse. I talked to the Postmaster who called a knowledgeable woman and then gave me directions to her house. I drove the twelve miles to the house of Mrs. Johnette King in forty-five minutes and was rewarded with her offer to accompany me the rest of the way to the Austin log school-house. Once we got to the site, we pulled off the road a few hundred feet and stopped in the brush. As we were getting out of the car, Mrs. King whispered that I freeze and slowly turn my head. Before us was an elk with her two young. In a few seconds, they got our scent and took off into the forest.

Of the 125 schools I have managed to photograph, the smallest is the Cottonwoods school, situated on the plantation of the same name. Located in Pulaski County and owned by Pemberton McRae, it was built in 1902 for the Pembertons' children. It measures about ten feet by sixteen feet and is painted plantation green with white trim. Inside, the wall studs are exposed, and the blackboard had been removed, and there are only two old school benches. But it still looks just right, nestled in the countryside with the other farm buildings.

As is probably obvious from the photographs, most of the Arkansas schoolhouses are constructed of milled boards. A few are native fieldstone, brick, or hand-hewn logs. One log school has its original hand-hewn wood door. When it was first built, the floor sills rested on one or more large stones. In time the space between them was filled with loose stones and mortar, keeping the floor warmer in cold months and helping to keep out animals. The schools of stone are of later vintage and were built during the days of the Works Progress Administration (WPA) in the 1930s and

1940s. The cave at Ravenden Springs is a "found" shelter which was put to good use. Most of the earlier schoolhouses were destroyed by fire, by natural disaster, or by people. Many of the schoolhouses have also seen other uses, as churches, community centers, barns, or residences, and many are now in disrepair or near collapse. Few of these buildings are the "little red" or "little white" schoolhouse we usually think of. Although most of the schoolhouses pictured here are literally "one-room" schoolhouses, I have chosen to include a few that have two rooms, and these are designated in the text.

In trying to capture the schoolhouses on film, I was primarily concerned with how to catch them in the best light. Once I located a schoolhouse I wanted to photograph, the problem of getting close enough often meant climbing through high brush, negotiating a barbed wire fence, or climbing a steep embankment. I then looked for the angle that revealed the most distinctive characteristics of the building. Solving that problem sometimes presented the next: trees or bushes blocked the view. In these cases, I had to return in the winter after the vegetation had fallen away. Even then the building was sometimes so completely obscured that only a small portion was visible.

All of the photographs in this book were made with cameras fitted with a pinhole. Two of the cameras were constructed by hand, and one was modified by attaching a pinhole disk on a glass lens.

The pinhole camera is a very simple device which can be made using ordinary household objects. A shoebox or oatmeal cylinder painted black inside, a needle, black tape, and a piece of aluminum foil or black paper can be assembled to form a tube camera. A small hole is cut in the center of one end of the box and a carefully-pierced piece of foil taped over the inside of the box. The shutter is constructed by covering the outside hole of the box with a flap of black tape, hinged so it can be partially lifted to expose the film.

The different effects achieved in these photographs were a direct result of using pinhole cameras. Although they function in much the same way as a standard camera—letting focused light be projected into a black box against a plane of sensitized film for a certain duration—other aspects of a pinhole camera are decidedly non-standard.

When light rays pass through a very small hole, or aperture, they take on the configuration of the hole and spread out in a cone, becoming larger as they recede from the hole to the plane of the film. The distance from the aperture to the film plane is known as the focal length. As the focal length increases, the cones overlap causing the image to be less sharp, even fuzzy. However, there are several formulas that may be used to figure the proper pinhole size for any focal length in order to get a high resolution image. With a short focal length, the light rays do not travel as far and therefore do not overlap as much, thus producing a sharper image. As the focal length becomes shorter, however, the image will be smaller.

The light rays that travel straight through the pinhole reach the film first which allows for very little overlapping. This accounts for the center being the sharpest portion of the image. It follows, therefore, that those passing through the pinhole from the edge of the scene become increasingly distorted. Since less light passes through the edges they will also be darker. The overall effect of using a wide-angle pinhole is that the picture grows gradually darker and more distorted as it moves away from the center.

The tube camera—which was used only for the photograph of Robert's Gap—produces the most distortion. With this camera the film was wrapped around the inside of the tube, leaving just enough space between the edges of the film so as not to cover the pinhole. The action of the light rays is the same as with a normal or wide-angle camera except that the tube causes the rays to fall on a cylindrical plane. This obviously results in distortion which is exacerbated when the film is laid flat for printing, although the center portion of the image remains nearly normal.

As I neared the end of my project, I decided to try recording some of the structures using a pinhole behind a glass lens. Since a glass lens bends the light passing through it to a point of focus, I knew that it would give a sharper image than a regular pinhole does, but I did not realize that it would make as great a difference as it did. My hope was that the clarity of the image would fall somewhere between that of the standard glass lens camera and the regular pinhole.

I started photographing one-room schoolhouses in 1985; most of these photographs were taken between 1989 and 1992. The purpose of this book, however, is not to offer a detailed historical document. Rather, it is to share a vision of these special buildings that were so important in shaping our educational system, communities, and lives.

Although this project has the earmarks of a solo endeavor, it was only realized because of the help and effort of a diverse group of good and generous people.

One day at lunch in 1989, Cyrus Sutherland, professor emeritus of architecture, University of Arkansas, Fayetteville, suggested that I photograph early one-room schools in Arkansas with my pinhole cameras. The possibility of publishing a book did not occur until several months later, at which time he advised me to contact the people at the Arkansas Historic Preservation Program in Little Rock for information. I am extremely grateful for his counsel.

I wish to thank several people from the Arkansas Historic Preservation Program: Cathryn H. Buford, director, and Kenneth Grunewald, deputy director, for their help and consideration regarding funding for this book, and Kenneth Storey and Patrick Zollner, architectural historians. Thanks also to Barbara Lindsey-Allen, survey coordinator, and Todd Ferguson, survey historian, for their cheerful research and professional guidance.

Special thanks also goes to Arkansas Power and Light and to Kay Kelley Arnold, AP&L vice president, communications, and to Entergy Corporation and Jerry Maulden, without whose effort this project would not have come about.

And finally, thanks are due to T. Harri Baker of the University of Arkansas at Little Rock History Department, to Dorothy Messick for her hospitality, to Mary Anne Miller for her typing, to Sally Ann Williams for her typing and encouragement, and to all the good folks at the University of Arkansas Press for all their good work.

Thomas Harding
March 1992

The Photographs

Amos

This old wood-frame schoolhouse is just off Surrey Road in the Lakeview community (Baxter County) and is difficult to see from the road. The bell tower and a portion of the original roof can be seen above the lower roof line which has been added to the front as has another room. The interior contained old furniture and automobile parts and was in a state of disrepair. At one time the structure was used as a Free Will Baptist Church. No construction data were available.

Arkana

This old schoolhouse is located on Highway 201, about twelve miles south of Mountain Home in Baxter County. According to Armel Hughes of Mountain Home, the structure was built between 1884 and 1886. This is unusual since very few two-room schools were constructed before 1900. During World War II, a lean-to, which housed a large fireplace and a hand-pump water well, was added to the right side. According to Mr. Hughes the lean-to was used as a place for canning vegetables. The schoolhouse has a stone foundation, weatherboard siding, and a metal hip roof with a brick chimney in the center. The gable in the front may have housed a bell. The long front-porch wall has four door openings, two for each classroom. Trash is scattered about the interior.

Austin

This log schoolhouse sits about two hundred yards off Highway 389, on a dirt road, some twelve miles west of Scotland (Van Buren County), deep in the Ozark National Forest. The structure is made of long, round logs and has a metal roof. The windows are unusually high and very small. The door was locked, but peering through a small opening, I could see several very dirty old mattresses and some furniture scattered about. There was no way to determine the building's age nor to secure any historical data.

Bald Tom

A dirt road out from the Clarkridge community
(Baxter County) leads to this small native stone schoolhouse.
None of the neighbors was available for information but the following was written in the concrete lintel over the door and cornerstone: "Dist. 12 Built May 1935. Members of School Board—
E. Trivett (Uncle Lige), W. R. Thatcher, Ernest Chandler, H. W.
Stone, Contractor." Some of the large stones in the wall are com-
posed of unusual crystal formations that resemble vari-colored
foam bubbles. Above the door is a rectangular concrete block
with small rocks embedded, forming the letters "B.T." The building is now used as a residence, and a small frame addition has
been added to one side.

Big Creek

This stone structure, which can be seen from about one-quarter of a mile away, is located about six miles south of Mammoth Spring in Fulton County, on property owned by Arch Waits. Mr. Waits offered to go with me because the terrain was quite rough. As we went, he told me that in 1985 vandals did extensive damage to the bell tower, destroyed the bell, and broke holes in the solid limestone walls. Since the school was badly damaged there has been little interest in restoring it. It is now used as a hay barn. The school was in District 101 and was built in 1910.

Big Four

This building, which at one time was used to store hay, is located on a dirt road in the vicinity of Providence in White County. High brush and tall grass obscured the view of it from the road. Built in 1915 and remodeled by the WPA in 1930, this two-room schoolhouse is framed with weatherboard novelty siding. The foundation is stone and the roof is covered with composition shingles. The windows are all on the back wall and there are two doors on the front. A wall with a doorway separates the two rooms. One of the rooms has a proscenium arch over a raised stage cluttered with dusty lumber. On the floor below the stage is an old piano. The other room has a large blackboard covered with graffiti, and there are still a few pieces of chalk in the rail. An old bench and desk are the only other furnishings.

Boxley

This photograph of the imposing Boxley school
(Newton County) was made in early spring of 1985. Constructed in
1899, the building housed on the lower floor the school originally
known as Walnut Grove, while the second floor was used as a meet-
ing place for a lodge. Church services are now held on the first floor.
A cemetery sits beside the school.

Brown

The location of this old schoolhouse was given to me by Carolyn Marshall and Fred Garcia, both National Park Service rangers at Tyler Bend (Searcy County) on the Buffalo River. The building is about four miles from the information center, in the forest on a very narrow dirt road. Cane Creek must be forded about 150 to 200 feet downstream, and small cars and recreational vehicles should not try to cross.

The exterior is drop siding, possibly painted white at one time. There are two windows on each side of the building. It has a metal roof and a belfry. The interior has a tongue-and-groove wood floor, with a raised platform at the front end. A stovepipe is visible in the ceiling. Interior walls are ten-inch boards.

According to the rangers the structure was moved from its original location by the flooding of Cane Creek in 1982. It was swept from its original foundation and swung around 90 degrees, finally lodging against a tree. As one area resident put it, "It floated up in the hills."

Elisha Brown is said to have donated the land for the school and may be responsible for its name. Most local residents know the structure as "Pap Brown School." However, the name School District No. 4 and Brown School appear on county records. Brown School was listed on the Searcy County tax records in 1882 and served families from the Calf Creek to Tyler Bend. The construction date is unknown.

In the unpublished *History and Folklore of Searcy County*, Ava Work said, "I was five years old when I started to Brown School on Lower Calf Creek near Arnold Bend. That was in 1915, the year the schoolhouse was built for that term."

Buford

This old schoolhouse is located at a private museum at Bull Shoals (Marion County). Its original name was Buford School, now called "Mountain Village School." Construction date was 1889. The white building seems to peek out from the large oak trees surrounding it. My first impression on seeing the structure was one of sheer elation. Buck Gascon, the owner, unlocked the door, said goodbye, and left. The interior was spotless; everything was as I had hoped—the blackboard, teacher's desk, the old stove and flue. But I suppose what impressed me most were the pupils' desks. They were all handmade by local people and surprisingly none had an inkwell hole.

Burnt

Mrs. D. Messick of Mountain Home accompanied me when I was trying to locate this school near Lone Rock community in Baxter County. Mrs. Messick had asked several members of the Baxter County Historical Society (of which she was program chair in 1990) for any historical information about the building which is now used as a church. This was to no avail. I've used the name "Burnt" because the exterior board and battens look as though they have been burned. Some of the windows are original.

Byron

This old schoolhouse is in Byron, some twelve miles southwest of Salem (Fulton County) on Highway 395. It is a two-room L-shaped structure. Notes from *Fulton County History*, compiled by Vester Williams, state that one Garrett Hunter was the first settler in the Byron community, arriving in the late 1840s. The first public school was established in 1869. Classes were taught from the first through the eighth grades. The original building was a one-room log structure, now gone. In 1900 a new one-room school was built (that with the large gable on the right). Then, in 1923, another room was added to the left. The original name for the school was "Mountain Grove at Byron." The structure, now a hay barn, has stone piers, weatherboard siding, metal roof, and a brick chimney at the rear. All are in very poor condition.

Capps

About one mile off of Highway 106 in the Capps community (Boone County) sits this beautiful two-room schoolhouse. It was built in 1917 on land donated by Mr. Capps, after whom it was named. The building has a continuous foundation, weatherboard siding, and a metal hipped roof with an interior brick central chimney. On the front of the building there is a bell tower with a bell. The schoolhouse is now used as a community building and is the object of an excellent job of restoration and maintenance. This is a rear elevation shot.

Cave

According to *History of Randolph County* by
Lawrence Dalton, this cave is reputed to be the first school in
Arkansas and was organized by Professor Caleb Lindsey. The cave
is in a gorge that runs through the town of Ravenden Springs and,
because of the loose rocks and sharp angle of the gorge walls, is
somewhat difficult to reach. The temperature was well below freez-
ing on the morning I drove from Little Rock to Ravenden Springs.
Had it not been for a young couple who helped me, I would not
have been able to find the cave nor to negotiate the descent. The
small stream at the bottom was partially frozen over, and the pro-
truding rocks were covered with ice. Several years ago a wooden
barrier covered the mouth of the cave but has since been replaced
by a concrete wall that does not completely cover the opening.
However, it was impossible to climb up to see inside the cave.
Etched in the concrete is the information that the school there was
organized by Professor Lindsey. After I took the picture, the three
of us were able to crawl through a small opening near the mouth of
the cave and locate a less hazardous route to the top of the gorge.

Coates

This delightful, small structure is located near south Maysville (Benton County), and according to Morris Loux, was built in 1915 by B. Holland and D. Ketchum. The walls are of cast concrete blocks and fashioned quoins. The eaves are of wooden shingles. Originally built as a school, it is now used as a family and community chapel. A cemetery is located nearby.

Colord

Across the railroad tracks in Beebe (White County) sits this small abandoned brick building. It was built for black children in 1944 by Gilbreath and Swan to replace an old school building, which was torn down. Mrs. Houston Hill, who lives nearby, said she went to school in the original schoolhouse. She showed me a group photograph of the teacher and his students standing in front of the building. Even though only a small portion of the original building was visible, it was obviously more elegant than this one. The school housed grades one through eight. Mrs. Hill, who was seventy-eight when we spoke, attended school there through the fourth grade. It was a residence later, and there still remain a tub and other fixtures.

Cottonwoods

Located on the Pulaski-Lonoke county line near Scott is the Pemberton Plantation. It is now owned by Pemberton McRae, grandson of the original owner. This playhouse-like school measures about ten feet by sixteen feet and was constructed in 1902 as a school for the Pemberton children. Its walls are of 1" x 10" rough board and batten, which are stained Plantation Green on the outside and left as exposed studs on the inside. Having been moved from its original site, it now rests on concrete blocks. Two desks remain inside, sheltered by the corrugated metal roof. The blackboard has been removed.

Dog Branch

This stone school building with a metal roof, located near Osage (Carroll County), was built in the late 1800s. The bell is outside on non-original stone supports. Now used as a church, the building adjoins a well-kept cemetery. The photo was made in the rain.

Dutton

After turning off Highway 16 onto a dirt road for about one-eighth of a mile, one approaches the Glen Parker Ranch in Madison County. Partially hidden by trees and other foliage is the large and imposing Dutton schoolhouse. Considering that it was built in 1890 and has not been used since the mid-1940s, it is in surprisingly good condition. The large schoolroom still has perhaps fifteen student desks, although they are not the original ones. As I walked with Mr. Parker toward the front beneath the bell tower, he reached for the rope and pulled it a couple of times ringing the bell which sounded beautiful. He explained that the bell is now used in emergencies, such as fire or severe weather conditions, and that the building is used occasionally for community meetings.

Eakins

After making inquiries along Highway 27, I stopped at the Ozark National Forest facility to ask if they knew of any one-room schoolhouses. The ranger made several calls and referred me to an older man at Nogo, a community in Pope County, eighteen to twenty miles up the road from Hector. Unfortunately, this man could give me no information other than that the building was "just up the road on my left." The building has asphalt brick siding and a metal roof. The frame construction appeared ready to collapse.

Fairmount

Twelve miles south of Hazen (Prairie County) on Highway 11 sits this handsome white schoolhouse with its well-proportioned bell tower. The land was donated by the Harr family, and the building was erected in 1910 as a two-room school. Mrs. Dorothy Harr, who is a trustee, gave me a tour of the structure which is now a community building. The exterior walls are novelty siding. Concrete piers form the foundation. The bell tower contains the original bell which cannot be rung because the rope is broken. The well with its hand pump stands a few paces away from the building. A small addition was added to the front which did away with the front door, and a side door was added. The partition separating the two classrooms was taken out. A covered hole in the ceiling indicates where the stove had been. Grades went from first through eighth.

Fluty

This old schoolhouse is located in Baxter County about twenty miles northeast of Mountain Home, near Fluty Chapel on land donated by a Civil War captain named Fluty. The schoolhouse was erected in 1904, but is not the original Fluty School. The original name was District 1. The building has been so badly damaged by the elements and vandals that the floor is unsafe to walk on. On the far wall is a blackboard, consisting of boards painted black which are separated by a cabinet. Suspended above the narrow cabinet is the flue, which had a pipe going out from the stove in the middle of the room. The cabinet was used to store library books, I was told by Mrs. Rixie G. Hicks who lives nearby and owns the property. Mrs. Hicks said she is very distressed that she cannot afford to have even minor repairs made.

Garrett Creek

This log schoolhouse is situated in the Prairie Grove Battlefield State Park at Prairie Grove (Washington County), twelve miles west of Fayetteville on Highway 62. It was moved to this location in the late 1950s from Cove Creek, which is about sixteen miles south of Prairie Grove.

Before the Civil War a pole-log school building was erected on Cove Creek. It was called Wilburn School after the people who owned the land. About 1870 high water washed the building away. A replacement schoolhouse, built on higher ground near Garrett Creek, burned in 1891. The next school term was held in the runway of Uncle Ob Pierce's barn. There is no record of when work on a new building was begun, but Harrison Pierce remembers seeing work underway in 1897 (*Prairie Grove Enterprise*, August 27, 1959).

The small schoolhouse of hand-hewn logs now rests on a continuous stone foundation. The roof and eaves are of wood shakes. The brick chimney was built by Will Clines and Riley Quinton in 1925. The teacher's desk, which was built in 1921 by Jeff Cantrell, sits on a wood platform. The teacher's salary was fifty dollars per month in 1928 and 1929 for the four-month school term. There were fourteen pupils in grades one through eight.

Gid

About ten miles north of Guion (Izard County), on Highway 58, a dirt road runs to the east for nearly a half mile and there sit the remains of this old schoolhouse, with its well close by. The schoolhouse is located in a cow lot, and the building itself serves as a hay barn. It is full of hay bales, and thus very little could be seen of the interior. Built about 1900, the foundation is stone as are the high steps to the covered porch. The frame construction is covered by shiplap siding, and the roof is corrugated metal. Particle board covers some openings. No history was available.

Gravel Hill

The ruins of this stone and brick building in White County along with its well house can be seen from the highway. I could find out nothing of its history. It could have been a two-room school, but with the roof and interior rooms caved in, there was no way to tell. It was probably abandoned in the 1940s because of school consolidation. No cornerstone was visible. The well house was in reasonably good condition, but the pump was gone.

Greenwood

Situated near Combs on Highway 295 near Greasy Creek (Madison County), this schoolhouse is surrounded by a fence and faces away from the road. Built in 1892, the structure is in good condition, especially the interior, and it is very clean and neat. I had heard that Orval Faubus has some connection with the old school, and when I reached him, the former governor told me that he had taught there, as had Harvey Combs, the insurance commissioner in his administration. The building is frame with a rock foundation. The desks are probably not original. Above the blackboard is a list of the names of the teachers and the dates they taught there.

Health

The remains of the Health schoolhouse are located approximately eleven miles south of Crosses (Madison County) on Highway 295. It is not easy to locate because of the trees and underbrush. Built about 1915, it has frame construction with novelty siding, stone foundation, and metal roof. No historical data were available.

Highland

This schoolhouse is located in the vicinity of
Highland on a dirt road off Highway 26 in Pike County. The
structure was built around 1920 to serve primarily the children of
the peach growers in that area. Judging by its size, it appears to
have been a two-room schoolhouse, but no historical data were
available. The front wall is the only one still standing, because when
the wood-shingle roof collapsed it took the other three walls with it.
The siding was weatherboards, and the foundation was stone piers.

Hulsey Bend

This schoolhouse, on Bill Freeze's farm near Oil Trough in Independence County, was built in 1900. The dark red building, trimmed in white, can be seen from a mile or so away. There is a weathered flagpole, with a tattered "Old Glory" waving, and a hand pump off to the side of the building. The old sign over one of the doors states: "Hulsey Bend School District 95 Est. 1898 Bldg Built 1900." In addition to the teacher's and students' desks, the room contains a foot organ, water keg, an old stove, book shelves, and a lady's horse saddle used by the teacher when she rode to school.

Hurricane

This photograph is not of the original school, which was destroyed by fire. A second building was blown down by a tornado. They were both named "Hickory Grove." The present building, built about 1932, is called "Hurricane," and is on the edge of a beautiful prairie in Prairie County. The land is owned by Mr. Gray. The building has an unusual recessed front, which frames the two entrance doors. The interior was completely filled with hay.

Idlewild

This delightful schoolhouse is located about two miles south of De Valls Bluff (Prairie County) on Highway 38. Built in 1921, the school rests on concrete piers. The construction is wood frame painted white. It has a bell tower at the front, and the bell still works. A brick flue is located at the far end of the building. A concrete walk leads to a covered porch which extends the width of the building. The roof is covered with composition shingles.

I quote from an article by Marie Price of De Valls Bluff: "The first Idlewild School burned. It was rumored that a teacher named it Idlewild because her pupils were idle and wild." The school was consolidated with De Valls Bluff in the 1940s, and the structure now serves as a community building. In 1972, a group of neighbors decided to refurbish it, and they did an exceptionally fine job.

Independence

This one-room schoolhouse, also known as the Prairie School, is located on the grounds of the Arkansas County Agricultural Museum in Stuttgart (Arkansas County). The original school, constructed in the 1880s, was blown down during a storm. It was replaced by this structure in 1914.

The original schoolhouse was located near Bayou Meto. It was organized by six or seven families who financed it without state or county funds. They named it the "Independent School." Later when it became part of the county school system, the name was changed to "Independence School."

When the county schools were closed, Frank Erstine bought the existing structure and moved it to his farm where it was used for grain storage. When he died his family gave the schoolhouse to the museum. It was moved to the museum grounds in 1975.

The building walls are wood siding painted red; the trim is white. The foundation is concrete piers, and the roof is covered with composition shingles. Windows are along the two side walls, and there are two separate front doors, one for boys and one for girls. In the classroom the two sexes were seated separately. The teacher's platform is at the far end of the building and at times was used as a stage. In the photograph can be seen a "three-holer" privy; usually there were only two, one for boys and one for girls.

Luber

This fieldstone structure is roughly twelve miles south of East Richwoods (Stone County), near the Luber community, on a dirt road. Construction date was about 1935. The floor is concrete and may not be the original. The west wall is the only one with windows. The roof is of corrugated metal, as is the porch roof. The teacher's platform is at one end, while the blackboard is along the east wall. Blending into one of the stone porch columns are small stones forming the initials of the builder, Thurmon Anderson. This well-maintained schoolhouse is now used as a community center. A dry wall extends around about three-fourths of the property, with the ruins of the well nearby to the east. Across the road behind are the remains of two outhouses.

Maple Springs

This small building is located on Crow Mountain on Teeter Road in the vicinity of Mars Hill (Pope County). It is situated on church property. The only information I could get about it was from a man who said he thought it was built around 1900. I could not see inside.

Marcella

Behind the Thomas Hess house in Stone County sits the old Marcella log schoolhouse. The actual construction date is unknown, but according to Jerry Jones, who lives in the Hess house, the school was built well before the turn of the century. The logs are large and hand hewn with square-notched corners. It is now used as a hay barn.

Oak Bluff

This 1899 school building is in the Skillet community, six miles from Sulphur Rock (Independence County). The exterior is in very good condition. Because the door was locked, I could not tell much about the interior. A sign on a tree said it was a "Coon Club." The bell was stolen a year or two ago.

Oak Grove

Sometimes called "Heel String," this structure is
located east of present Highway 223 on old Sturkie Road near Viola
in Fulton County. Originally, classes were held in a wood-frame
structure. However, in 1918 or 1919 it was replaced by this molded-
rock building by Uncle Ed Brown. It is now a dwelling.

Ozark Folk Center

Nestled among other buildings at the Ozark Folk Center near Mountain View (Stone County) is this small hand-hewn white-oak log schoolhouse. It was built in 1870 as a homestead in the Gaylor community of District 56 and served as a school, grades one through twelve, until the late 1920s. The students sat on split-log benches. These have been replaced with more modern desks. Classes were held for two and a half months each year. The Folk Center added the wood floor and replaced the roof. The school-house has been attractively furnished with various authentic objects of the time.

Patterson Springs

This schoolhouse is located in the vicinity of Oark (Johnson County), adjoining a cemetery, and was somewhat difficult for me to find. This neat, white, well-kept structure has a most unusual façade. The front wall is recessed and extends the width of the building, shielding the double doors in the center from the elements. The doors extend almost to the ground and are held shut by a large rock; there is no lock and key. The windows are covered with wood shutters. There is a new metal roof, and the walls are weatherboard. Inside is the usual raised platform, above and behind of which is the blackboard. Wood benches were stacked along the side walls when I was there. The cemetery nearby indicates that the old school is now being used as a church and possibly a community building. Arkansas Historic Preservation Program files show the construction date as about 1920.

Pension Mountain

This marvelously preserved little red schoolhouse is located in the Cabanal vicinity, some ten miles south of Berryville (Carroll County) on Pension Mountain. I was captivated by the exquisite toy-like structure sitting peacefully amid beautiful oak and pine trees. The walls are novelty siding, but vertical boards are visible under the current siding, and square nails can be seen. The white shutters on the windows were probably added later. The roof is metal, and the building rests on stone piers. Construction date was about 1890. I could not see inside since the door was locked and the windows were covered.

Pirouge

This old schoolhouse was built in 1905 and is in the
deep woods, seven and a half miles down a very rough dirt road off
Highway 56, between the towns of 44 and Band Mill (Izard County)
This structure is unique because of the steep, narrow steps and the
handrails with balusters. Peering inside, I could see only some mattresses and a stove.

Robert's Gap

This little schoolhouse is located near Boxley
(Newton County), about six miles from Highway 21 on a dirt
road up Cave Mountain. I passed probably four houses and a
church on the way up the mountain, and no one could give me
any historical background on the school. Upon going inside, I saw
an old piano in one corner on a raised platform. The blackboard
stretching across the width of the room was still in good condition.
Piles of dead leaves were on the floor, blown in through the open
door and broken windows. There was a hole in the ceiling for the
flue, but it was long gone, as was the wood stove. All of the other
furniture was missing. I suppose at some time it could have been a
church or community building, but I saw no evidence of it.

Rocky Branch
(Harrel)

Back in the tall grass off Highway 160 south of
Harrell (Calhoun County) sit the remains of the Rocky Branch
schoolhouse, which is in a pitiful state of repair. You can see the sky
through the roof openings where wood shingles had been. The
doors and windows are all removed; the board-and-batten walls are
warped and weathered. The suspended brick chimney is about to
cave in. The only bit of history I could find out about the building
was that it was built about 1910.

Rocky Branch (LaRue)

This Rocky Branch schoolhouse is located at Rocky Branch in Benton County off Highway 303 east of Rogers. It is a large white building with the school bell suspended under a four-sided pyramid roof that is supported by four posts. The construction is frame with wood siding and a composition-shingle roof. On the raised platform at the far end is the teacher's desk, a piano, and a bookcase. The blackboard appears to be the original one, and the wood stove still works. The schoolhouse was built about 1905 on the Loftis McGinnes farm, located about a mile and a half north of the school's present location.

When I first began searching for this school, I could not locate the LaRue community. With the help of a staff member of the Rogers Historical Museum who contacted the Corps of Engineers, I discovered to my dismay that the area was now under Beaver Lake. However, she also determined that the building had been moved in 1962 to high ground near the Rocky Branch community. Mrs. Ella Mae Stell was responsible for the relocation, thus saving the schoolhouse from destruction under Beaver Lake.

Rosenwald

This rural two-room schoolhouse is located in Pike County on Highway 26 about two miles east of Delight. It was built in 1938 by the WPA and is now on the National Register of Historic Places. The building was constructed with the help of a grant from the Julius Rosenwald Fund as a school for blacks, although whites did attend. The Rosenwald Fund contributed significantly to furthering black education in the South. Classes were held for first through eighth grades. The structure has white novelty siding, the foundation is of continuous cast concrete, and the roof is covered with composition shingles. There is an inside toilet which must be entered from the outside. The schoolhouse is now used as a community building and is well cared for.

St. James

Off Highway 14 in the community of St. James (Stone County) stands this timeworn schoolhouse, which was built in 1902 as a replacement for the original 1880 structure. The handsome bell tower was destroyed in a storm. The present porch was added later. This is now a community building, and the old students' desks, which were handmade, are still used. The desk tops have the usual pen-knife scratches and carved initials. Mrs. Bessie Moore of Little Rock taught at the school for three summer sessions. She also bought the blackboard for the school, although it is no longer on the wall. The community is trying to raise funds to paint and repair the building.

Smyrna (Lower)

This small schoolhouse near Huntsville (Madison County) is perhaps the most vernacular construction of all the schools I've come across. Built in 1877, its log walls were hand hewn and have mitered corners and no nails were used in the construction. The rear of the building has a ladder that ascends to a handmade wooden door which opens to an attic. The present interior has a raised platform, a piano, some wooden benches, and a fifty-gallon drum that serves as a stove. The building is now used as a church. The log walls are exposed on the inside, and on the outside they have been chinked with cement mortar.

Treat

Don Hamilton of Little Rock owns property near this old schoolhouse and accompanied me in locating this building. It is good that he did. The building is located across Moccasin Creek on a dirt road, about seventeen miles north of Dover in Pope County. The structure was built about 1920 to replace the original building, which was called Ross School. Due to the elements and neglect, the old school collapsed sometime in the fall of 1991.

Weathers

This old schoolhouse, surrounded by tall weeds, trees, and vines, is located on the outskirts of Atkins (Pope County) on Highway 324. Mrs. Paul Sweeden of Atkins gave me the following information: The building was constructed in 1884 and was used as a school until 1920. After that date it was used by the local Church of Christ congregation. Later it was sold to the Pope family and was last used as a residence. It is unoccupied at this time. Mrs. Sweeden also said Mr. and Mrs. Hugh Kendrick and Mrs. Velma Judkin Fronabarger, who are now all in a nursing home, attended school there. The school served the first through the eighth grades.

Whiteley

On a dirt road in the vicinity of Boxley (Newton County) stands this old schoolhouse which was named after a family of early settlers who lived in the area. The structure is now owned and maintained by the National Park Service. The school was built about 1913. Its wood siding and stone foundation are in good condition, but the door and windows are missing, although the window openings are screened. The bell tower seems very tall and narrow. I could not determine whether it still contained the bell.

Afterword

Education does not demand a shelter or a teacher, chalkboards or desks or lunch boxes, or even books, although all of those things are tools that make learning easier and quicker. Humanity long ago discovered the importance of formal education, which was accomplished best by assembling the young in groups and housing them in a common space where an adult, who had presumably mastered the basics, imparted those tenets of civilized living (symbolized by the three "Rs") to them. The one-room school is the building block of educational architecture.

Whether or not the one-room school has European antecedents, it is difficult to find an institution more characteristic of nineteenth-century American culture. Even before formalized state education systems were organized, westward-moving pioneers, settlers, and farmsteaders built schoolhouses very soon after they had provided shelters for themselves and their farm animals. Often the multi-purpose schoolhouses served as churches. Just as the houses and farm buildings reflected a limited selection of building materials— logs, sod, rough-sawn lumber, fieldstone, and sometimes home-kilned brick—schoolhouses and churches reflect the same limitations in their architecture.

The architecture of small-town and rural America, residential or institutional, is primarily a reflection of the basic and fundamental values of American life—honest assessment of essential human needs, lack of pretention and excess in aesthetics, strong faith in the importance of family and in the nurturing and education of youth.

This photographic record of some of the fast-disappearing one-room school buildings in Arkansas employs a wonderfully basic pin-hole photographic technique, which seems to be an extraordinarily appropriate medium to illustrate a wonderfully basic architectural form.

The "one-room" modifier leaves no doubt about the building's architectural plan. There is little question about its basic form. There seems to have been an unquestioned community image of what the school should look like: a gabled rectangle twenty to thirty feet in width, forty to fifty feet long, lighted on each side by four double-hung windows, sometimes six, sometimes only two or three. The building was entered at one end, most often through a single door recessed into its wall or sheltered by a small, projecting gabled stoop.

Almost as common was an entry of two doors, separated by six or eight feet, popularly regarded as a device for gender separation when students lined up after recess for an orderly reentry. This double-door entry seemed more common when the building doubled as a church and could have been inherited from an early church from which the traditionally required gender segregation during services carried over to entry and exit from the building. The twin doors may also have represented location of aisles between seating arrangements within the one-room interior.

Whatever the entry arrangement, the one-room school was more often than not a multipurpose building, serving, as the community or regional population grew, other functions in addition to the religious ones—as a voting precinct,or as a location for fund-raising pie suppers, funerals, weddings, and Christmas and other seasonal parties.

It is my belief that there were patterns of behavior and procedure unique to the one-room school, procedural patterns which resulted from the wide age spread among the pupils, from the presence of only one teacher to supervise the entire operation, from the generally austere facilities which lacked almost entirely those educational amenities now taken for granted in larger consolidated schools that have the added advantage of large specialized teaching faculties.

Having little personal experience with one-room schools, I wrote an invitation in a small-town Arkansas newspaper for some testimony of anyone who had attended or taught in a one-room school. There was a modest but important response to the invitation.

Mrs. Reppie Smith of Sapulpa, Oklahoma, wrote:

> Memories of my education in a one-room schoolhouse in Arkansas are very many and dear to me. And I do remember most everything.
>
> I started at age six in 1914 and finished the eighth grade in 1922. First through eighth grades were taught to about thirty or more students.
>
> The school was Liberty in a little town called Woolsey now. When I was growing up it was called Pitkin. There were two stores, the Pitkin post office, and Liberty School.
>
> The first graders started to learn their ABCs and numbers from a large chart. Later we received our first book: *The Primer*. From there we were learning words and some arithmetic.
>
> Reading, writing, arithmetic, history, spelling, grammar, geography, and penmanship were taught. Of course, the names of some of these subjects have been changed. Spelling and ciphering contests were usually held after the last recess on Fridays.
>
> I don't remember us ever taking school work home to study at night. Coal oil lamps didn't give out much light to study by.
>
> If our teachers had problems teaching that many children in a one-room space or with all the different classes, we didn't know anything about them. If we weren't reciting, we were busy getting our next lesson.
>
> The county superintendent came about twice each year (unannounced) to visit. My first grade teacher was Mrs. Hadsell. Later ones were Mr. Thrasher, Lillian_____ , Nora (Robinson) Karnes, and Mary (McGee) Skelton. Some taught two terms.

Our heating system was a woodburning box heater. Later it was replaced with an upright heater. This one had an outer jacket of heavy metal. This was for circulation. It was located at the back of the room in the corner.

If I remember right, it was the teacher's job to start the fire when they arrived at the schoolhouse much earlier than time for the children. Older boys brought in wood through the day and they kept the fire going. Our air conditioner was open windows. There were lots of windows and you sure could tell this come winter time.

The water we had to drink came from a hand-dug well. The well was on school property. Water was drawn up by bucket, rope, and pulley. Everyone had their own drinking cups. Some were tin and some were the folding kind. If you had a folding cup, you felt rich. The bucket of water was set on a shelf at the back. Older children kept the water ready for the rest of us.

We had a cloak room for coats, hats, and scarfs. A shelf in this little room held our lunches (lard or syrup buckets).

Now, about our rest room. It sat out back. It was nice and roomy. It was much nicer than I had at home. It had three seats you could rest on.

Repairs to the building, wood supply, chalk, and such were paid for by the school district.

My dad, A. M. Goff, was on the school board for several years. The wood-frame building blew down after I finished school. A concrete block one now stands in about the same place. It is used for church and community meetings (I think).

Mrs. Smith's essay covered all the bases. Hers was one of hundreds of one-room schools in Arkansas. I am certain Mrs. Smith's account would describe very accurately almost any one of those schools picked at random. I am equally certain that each one, over the century when such schools were active, would also have had a certain individual identity.

Mabel Goree Bell of Springdale, Arkansas, began her teaching career in Skylight School, District 116, Washington County, Arkansas, October 6, 1925—on her twentieth birthday.

I boarded with Mr. and Mrs. J. C. Glidewell. Mrs. Glidewell ran the country store. The first day of school Mr. Glidewell walked with me to the school to show me a short cut through the fields and under the fences.

The University of Arkansas had not taught me how to cope in a one-room school. One must learn that for oneself.

Skylight was a typical one-room school with a most notable exception. There were no school desks.

The school and church shared the building. The children sat on the church benches and wrote on their laps. The pupils from Primer through ninth grade took short turns on the recitation bench. Sometimes the older girls helped to teach the younger ones. There were several children in some families and the children were interested in hearing the others recite.

There was no electricity, no in-door plumbing, no running water, no school nurse, no playground equipment, no library, no hot lunches, no music teacher, no air-conditioning, no telephone, no school buses, no physical education instructor, no copy machine, no Venetian blinds, etc. Also there were no "snow" days and no "Me" days.

The children learned the basics. At the end of the six-month term three of the girls took the Washington County Teacher's Examination and passed.

In 1930 a petition was signed by the patrons asking that Skylight be consolidated with Mount Pleasant Morrow, District 44, in order to secure "standardized elementary High School facilities" for children of the territory.

There was a program at the end of school. The church let us use their organ. Some of the girls could play. So we had songs, plays and recreation.

I am thankful . . . to have had my teaching experience in a one-room school. I taught more than 30 years and Skylight was my first love. The children and parents were good, kind, gentle people and I have many happy memories.

Now there is school no more on Skylight Mountain.

Some districts were short-lived and were combined with others. Some rural districts survived until after World War II when state-wide consolidation literally deactivated the few one-room schools that remained. Though the one-room school is fast fading from memory, its importance to the social and educational heritage of Arkansas is undiminished. This book is a tribute to that heritage.

Cyrus Sutherland
March 1992

(Cyrus Sutherland is professor emeritus of architecture at the University of Arkansas, Fayetteville.)

Appendix

The camera I used to make most of these photographs was constructed by gluing together two pieces of 3/4-inch plywood. After cutting a hole in the plywood, I attached it to the back of an old 4" x 5" Speed Graphic camera. The front has a special type of air-release shutter with the brass pinhole attached to it. For a few of these pictures, I experimented with using a 35mm camera with a black metal pinhole disk placed between the lens elements.

I often use Polaroid Positive/Negative (Type 55) along with Ilford HP5 and Tri-X films (The last two are developed in HC 110). The images for this book were all printed on Ilford Multigrade stock and developed in Dektol. The f-stop for the 4" x 5" wide-angle camera is f128, the tube camera is f150, and the experimental one is f40. Exposure time for average sunlit buildings is two to twenty seconds, but some exposures for cloudy conditions or interiors are as long as twenty minutes. I use a tripod, exposure meter, and a special slide rule to determine exposures.

The following is a list of the schools featured in the preceding pages along with their approximate locations and the photographic methods used to achieve the results I did.

Amos (Lakeview, Baxter County): 4" x 5" wide-angle pinhole camera. Exposure with Tri-X film was for sixty seconds.
Arkana (Mountain Home, Baxter County): 4" x 5" wide-angle pinhole camera. Exposure with Tri-X film was for thirty seconds.
Austin (Scotland, Van Buren County): 4" x 5" wide-angle pinhole camera. Exposure with Tri-X film was for about forty-five seconds.

Bald Tom (Clarkridge, Baxter County): 4" x 5" wide-angle pinhole camera. Exposure with Tri-X film was for forty-five seconds.

Big Creek (Mammoth Spring, Fulton County): 4" x 5" wide-angle pinhole camera. Exposure was for thirty seconds using Tri-X film. The photo was made mid-morning.

Big Four (Providence, White County): 4" x 5" wide-angle pinhole camera. Exposure with Tri-X film was for six minutes.

Boxley (Boxley, Newton County): 4" x 5" wide-angle pinhole camera using a yellow filter. Exposure with Tri-X film was for twenty seconds.

Brown (Tyler Bend, Searcy County): 4" x 5" wide-angle pinhole camera. Exposure with Tri-X film was for sixty seconds.

Buford (Bull Shoals, Marion County): 4" x 5" wide-angle pinhole camera. Exposure with Tri-X film was for nine minutes.

Burnt (Lone Rock, Baxter County): 4" x 5" wide-angle pinhole camera. Exposure with Tri-X film was for thirty seconds.

Byron (Salem, Fulton County): 4" x 5" wide-angle pinhole camera. Exposure with Tri-X film was for two minutes.

Capps (Capps, Boone County): 4" x 5" wide-angle pinhole camera. Exposure with Tri-X film was for ten seconds.

Cave (Ravenden Springs, Randolph County): 4" x 5" wide-angle pinhole camera. Exposure was for one minute, using Ilford HP5 film.

Coates (Maysville, Benton County): 4" x 5" wide-angle pinhole camera. Exposure with Tri-X film was for twenty seconds.

Colord (Beebe, White County): 4" x 5" wide-angle pinhole camera. Exposure with Tri-X film was for twenty seconds.

Cottonwoods (Scott, Pulaski-Lonoke county line): 4" x 5"
                wide-angle pinhole camera. Exposure with Tri-X
                film was for twenty seconds.

Dog Branch (Osage, Carroll County): 4" x 5" wide-angle pinhole
                camera. Exposure with Polaroid Type 55 film was
                about six minutes.

Dutton (Dutton, Madison County): 4" x 5" wide-angle pinhole cam-
                era. Exposure with Tri-X film was for thirty seconds.

Eakins (Nogo, Pope County): 4" x 5" wide-angle pinhole camera.
                Exposure with Polaroid Type 55 film was for thirty
                seconds.

Fairmount (Hazen, Prairie County): 4" x 5" wide-angle pinhole
                camera. Exposure with Polaroid PN55 was for
                ninety seconds, using a red filter.

Fluty (Mountain Home, Baxter County): 4" x 5" wide-angle pin-
                hole camera. Exposure with Tri-X film was for
                ninety seconds.

Garrett Creek (originally at Cove Creek; now at Prairie Grove,
                Washington County): 4" x 5" wide-angle pinhole
                camera. Exposure with Tri-X film was for twelve
                minutes.

Gid (Guion, Izard County): Experimental 35mm pinhole camera.
                Exposure with Ilford HP5 film was for 1/2 second.

Gravel Hill (Gravel Hill, White County): Experimental 35mm pin-
                hole camera. Exposure with Ilford HP4 film was for
                1/2 second.

Greenwood (Combs, Madison County): 4" x 5" wide-angle pinhole
                camera. Exposure with Tri-X film was for sixteen
                minutes.

Health (Crosses, Madison County): 4" x 5" wide-angle pinhole cam-
                era. Exposure with Tri-X film was for one minute.

Highland (Highland, Pike County): 4" x 5" wide-angle pinhole cam-
                era. Exposure with Tri-X film was for thirty seconds.

Hulsey Bend (Oil Trough, Independence County): 4" x 5" wide-angle pinhole camera. Exposure with Tri-X film was one minute.

Hurricane (Prairie County): Experimental 35mm pinhole camera. Exposure with Ilford HP4 film was for seven seconds.

Idlewild (De Valls Bluff, Prairie County): 4" x 5" wide-angle pinhole camera. Exposure with Polaroid PN55 film was for 45 seconds.

Independence (originally at Bayou Meto; now at Stuttgart, Arkansas County): 4" x 5" wide-angle pinhole camera. Exposure with Tri-X film was for ten seconds.

Luber (East Richwoods, Stone County): 4" x 5" wide-angle pinhole camera. Exposure with Ilford HP4 film at for forty-five seconds.

Maple Springs (Mars Hill, Pope County): Experimental glass with pinhole f40 lens. Exposure with Ilford HP5 film was for one second.

Marcella (Marcella, Stone County): 4" x 5" wide-angle pinhole camera. Exposure with Tri-X film was for thirty seconds.

Oak Bluff (Sulphur Rock, Independence County): 4" x 5" wide-angle pinhole camera. Exposure with Tri-X film at for six minutes.

Oak Grove (Viola, Fulton County): 4" x 5" wide-angle pinhole camera. Exposure with Tri-X film was for about eight minutes. Taken during a rain shower.

Ozark Folk Center (originally at Gaylor; now at Mountain View, Stone County): 4" x 5" wide-angle pinhole camera. Exposure with Tri-X film was for five minutes.

Patterson Springs (Oark, Johnson County): 4" x 5" wide-angle pinhole camera. Exposure with Tri-X film was for one minute.

Pension Mountain (Berryville, Carroll County): 4" x 5" wide-angle pinhole camera. Exposure with Tri-X film was for about sixty seconds.

Pirouge (Band Mill, Izard County): 4" x 5" wide-angle pinhole camera. Exposure with Polaroid PN55 film was for eight minutes.

Robert's Gap (Boxley, Newton County): 4" x 5" tube pinhole camera. Exposure was for thirty seconds, using Ilford HP5 film.

Rocky Branch (Harrell, Calhoun County): 4" x 5" wide-angle pinhole camera. Exposure with Tri-X film was for thirty seconds.

Rocky Branch (originally at LaRue; now at Rogers, Benton County): 4" x 5" wide-angle pinhole camera. Exposure with Tri-X film was for one minute, forty-five seconds, using a sky filter.

Rosenwald (Delight, Pike County): 4" x 5" wide-angle pinhole camera. Exposure with Tri-X film was for forty-five seconds.

St. James (St. James, Stone County): 4" x 5" wide-angle pinhole camera. Exposure with Tri-X film was for thirty seconds.

Smyrna (Lower) (Huntsville, Madison County): 4" x 5" wide-angle pinhole camera. Exposure with Tri-X film was for sixty seconds.

Treat (Dover, Pope County): 4" x 5" wide-angle pinhole camera. Exposure with Tri-X film was for two minutes.

Weathers (Atkins, Pope County): Experimental 35mm pinhole camera. Exposure with Ilford HP5 film was for 1/2 second.

Whiteley (Boxley, Newton County): 4" x 5" wide-angle pinhole camera. Exposure with Tri-X film was for ninety seconds.